Wrestling Greats

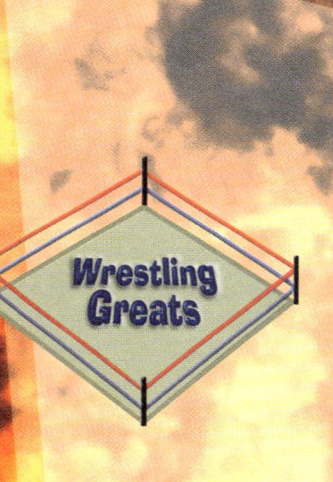

KEVIN NASH

Ross Davies

The Rosen Publishing Group, Inc.
New York

Published in 2002 by The Rosen Publishing Group, Inc.
29 East 21st Street, New York, NY 10010

Copyright © 2002 by The Rosen Publishing Group, Inc.

First Edition

All rights reserved. No part of this book may be reproduced in any form without permission in writing from the publisher, except by a reviewer.

Library of Congress Cataloging-in-Publication Data

Davies, Ross.
Kevin Nash / Ross Davies. — 1st ed.
p. cm. — (Wrestling greats)
Includes bibliographical references (p.) and index.
Summary: Discusses the life and matches of the wrestler Kevin Nash.
ISBN 0-8239-3492-6
1. Nash, Kevin, 1958– —Juvenile literature.
2. Wrestlers—United States—Biography—Juvenile literature.
[1. Nash, Kevin, 1958– 2. Wrestlers.]
I. Title. II. Series
GV1196.N37 D38 2001
796.812'092—dc21

2001002764

Manufactured in the United States of America

Contents

1 *A Wrestling Villain* — 5
2 *Growing Strong* — 12
3 *The Dark Days in WCW* — 23
4 *The Diesel Train* — 30
5 *The World Champion* — 45
6 *The New World Order* — 57
7 *One Becomes Two Becomes One* — 72
8 *Return to Superstardom* — 86
  Glossary — 100
  For More Information — 106
  For Further Reading — 108
  Index — 111

Nash started as a wrestler in WCW, then resurrected his career in the WWF before returning to WCW.

A Wrestling Villain

The headline took the wrestling world by storm. On June 10, 1996, the front page of *Pro Wrestling Illustrated Weekly* read "Razor Ramon Looking for Friends in World Championship Wrestling." According to the article, there was speculation that WWF wrestler Diesel would be one of those friends.

"You'll know who my friends are when I want you to know," Ramon said, refusing to give any clues.

But, in reality, wrestling fans had all the clues that they needed. Diesel and Ramon had been friends and then rivals in the World Wrestling Federation, but recently they had become friends again. They had formed an imposing tag team in 1996. Just a few months earlier, Diesel had announced that he was leaving the WWF and was returning to World Championship Wrestling.

For Diesel, this would be a return to the scene of past failures. In the early 1990s, the man born Kevin Nash had wrestled in WCW under several names, including Master Blaster Steel, Oz, and Vinnie Vegas. No matter which alter ego Nash used, he lost most of his matches.

A Wrestling Villain

However, his career took off when he moved to the WWF in 1993. He won the world tag team, intercontinental, and world heavyweight titles, and he was rated the number one wrestler in the world. Regardless, Nash wanted to return to WCW in order to prove that his WWF successes were not flukes.

The questions about Ramon's friends were answered at WCW's Great American Bash just six days after the *Pro Wrestling Illustrated Weekly* headline appeared. Diesel and Ramon showed up at the Bash, confronted WCW senior vice president Eric Bischoff, and demanded a match against the three best wrestlers in WCW. When Bischoff told them that they would have to wait to find out who their opponents would be, Ramon punched Bischoff in the stomach, and Diesel power-bombed him through the stage.

Diesel and Ramon had been calling themselves the Outsiders—WWF invaders set on taking over WCW—but they reverted to calling themselves by their real names, Kevin Nash and Scott Hall. Over the following weeks, they learned that their opponents at the Bash at the Beach on July 7, 1996, in Daytona Beach, Florida, would be Sting, Lex Luger, and Randy Savage—three of WCW's hottest superstars. But Nash and Hall had a secret of their own: the identity of their third team member.

A Wrestling Villain

In fact, nobody knew the identity of the third Outsider until nearly the end of the match. Nash and Hall wrestled two-against-three for most of the match. Despite being outnumbered, Nash and Hall dominated the match and injured Luger. As Luger was being carried from the ring on a stretcher, Hulk Hogan—perhaps the most famous and most popular wrestler ever—walked down the aisle.

The television announcers and most of the fans thought that he was there to help Sting and Savage, but instead Hogan climbed into the ring and started legdropping Savage, who was down on the mat. Then he high-fived

Nash and Hall. The crowd was shocked. Fans threw trash into the ring. As Hogan booed and yelled at the fans, Hall and Nash stood by and laughed.

"This is a dark day for wrestling," Sting said. "If you can't trust Hulk, who can you trust?"

Well, the fans certainly couldn't trust Hogan, and they couldn't trust Nash and Hall either. Nash, Hall, and Hogan declared that their new group was called the New World Order and that they planned on getting even bigger and more dangerous. Within months, the NWO would be on the verge of taking over WCW, and no wrestler would be safe from their attacks.

Kevin Nash's golden mane obscures his face as he grapples with an opponent.

As for Nash, the man who had revived his career as Diesel in the WWF was about to soar to new heights in WCW—even higher than his seven-foot frame. The NWO ruled the wrestling world. And Kevin Nash, who had grown up fantasizing about comic-book heroes and wrestling greats, was one of the biggest villains of all.

2 Growing Strong

Kevin Nash was born on July 9, 1958, in suburban Detroit, Michigan. His mother, Wanda, and his father, Robert, worked at the Ford Motor Company, which was not too far from their home. Although the Nashes were by no means rich, they were comfortable, and they had a wonderful family life. Kevin had an older brother, Mark, and a younger sister, Kim.

Robert Nash was a family man who enjoyed playing games with his children. According to *Wrestling True Life Stories Volume 2*, Robert loved playing toy soldiers with Kevin. Robert could be silly, goofy, and childish, but he was always fun, and his family always came first. Frequently, and on an impulse, Robert would pack his three children into the family car, drive to the ice-cream shop, and treat his children to as much ice cream as they wanted.

As much fun as the family had six days of the week, Sunday was reserved for church. The family never missed church, and religion was an important part of Kevin's life. After church, the family would go out to dinner and eat as much as they wanted. In the Nash family, nobody ever went hungry, and nobody ever felt unloved.

Kevin had two hobbies: comic books and pro wrestling. The fantasy aspect of both pastimes appealed to him, and he grew up daydreaming about his favorite comic-book characters and watching the great wrestlers of the time, such as Lou Thesz, Gene Kiniski, and Dick the Bruiser. Kevin's mother didn't like his fascination with wrestling and comic books, and she warned him to stay away from his uncle Chuck's house. It was at Uncle Chuck's that Kevin would watch wrestling on the black-and-white television and read his uncle's wrestling magazines.

Growing Strong

The fun of Kevin's early childhood ended in tragedy. Kevin was only eight years old when his father died of a heart attack at age thirty-six. After her husband's death, Wanda Nash returned to work at the Ford plant so she could support her family. She took what work she could get, sometimes working night shifts. Kevin, Mark, and Kim often had to stay with neighbors or relatives. In spite of Robert's death, Wanda was determined to make sure that her children would never go without food or proper clothing and that they would do well in school. Despite the upheaval, Wanda did her best to ensure that her children had everything they needed.

In 1968, two years after Robert died, Wanda remarried. Her second husband was Allan MacDonald, and he was as good a stepfather as the children could have ever hoped for. He treated them as if they were his own. Allan played football, baseball, and basketball with his new children, and soon they were even calling him "Dad."

Kevin had been a large baby at birth, and he grew rapidly throughout his adolescence. He was six feet ten inches tall

Growing Strong

by the age of fourteen, but unlike most extremely tall teenagers, he wasn't thin as a rail. He was solidly built, and he was very agile. He also had tremendous strength. All of these attributes made him a natural for the basketball court.

Kevin was so impressive on the basketball court that he made the varsity team at Trenton High in Detroit when he was a freshman, even though freshmen usually played junior varsity. With his mom—his most avid fan—watching from the bleachers, Kevin was a star player who dominated the local competition. In his senior year at Trenton, Kevin received offers to play basketball from nearly 200 colleges. Ultimately, he picked the University of

Kevin Nash

Tennessee, which was only eight hours from Detroit. Kevin wanted to go to a school where his mother could see him play.

Kevin played for the University of Tennessee Volunteers in 1978, 1979, and 1980, and he even played in the Sweet Sixteen, the regional semifinals, of the NCAA men's basketball tournament. During his career at Tennessee, he averaged 5.1 points and 4.2 rebounds per game. But things didn't always go smoothly. In 1980, during a loss to the University of Kentucky Wildcats, Kevin got into a shouting match with several Wildcats players. After the game, Kevin even got into a shouting match with Volunteers coach Don DeVoe. Kevin finished the 1979–1980 season his junior

Nash's natural ability as an athlete, combined with his ambition and hard work, enabled him to excel not only in wrestling but in basketball, too.

year, but did not return for his senior year. Instead, Kevin left school and played basketball in Germany for several years. He was even invited to a Cleveland Cavaliers training camp. He retired from basketball at age twenty-five because of a knee injury. The injury was so serious that doctors doubted whether he'd ever be able to play sports again.

Kevin returned home to Detroit and got an assembly line job at Ford. On weekends, he hung out with his friends. It seemed like Kevin was destined to live the life of a blue-collar worker, toiling on the assembly line for average wages. Then, one Friday night, Kevin and his friends went to Joe Louis Arena in downtown Detroit to

Growing Strong

watch the World Wrestling Federation. Sitting in a ringside seat, watching the pros, Kevin thought to himself, "I can do this."

After all, Kevin had everything he needed to become a star in pro wrestling: size and athletic ability. He was seven feet tall and weighed 355 pounds, and he towered over most other wrestlers. Kevin took immediate action. He moved to Atlanta—a hot spot of professional wrestling—and took a job as a nightclub bouncer. At the nightclub, he became friends with several professional wrestlers, including Barry Windham, Rick Steiner, and Scott Steiner. He started training at the Power Plant, a local wrestling school run by Jody Hamilton (also known as the Assassin).

Kevin lifted weights in the early morning, worked at the nightclub from 11 AM to 8 PM, and trained at the Power Plant at night. In 1990, Nash signed a contract with the National Wrestling Alliance (now known as World Championship Wrestling) and took on the ring name Steel. His teammate was Blade. They called themselves the Master Blasters.

And they lost one match after another.

The Dark Days in WCW

Master Blaster Steel certainly stood out in a crowd. He was seven feet tall, and he wore his hair in an orange mohawk. Both Steel and Blade wore colorful face makeup. As 1990 wore on, the Master Blasters started winning more than they lost, but promoters were in no hurry to grant them shots at the WCW world tag team title. Though they appeared on one pay-per-view event, Halloween Havoc on October 27, 1990, and beat the Southern Boys, they never received the title shots they coveted.

The truth is that most wrestlers aren't instant sensations. Men like Bill Goldberg, who battle for world titles within a year of making their debuts, are rare. Most wrestlers have to pay their dues by losing matches, wrestling lesser competitors, and proving their ability at arena shows that aren't televised. That's exactly what happened with Kevin Nash.

In 1991, the wrestling world was introduced to an unusual character named Oz. Ted Turner, who at the time owned CNN and TBS, among other cable TV networks, had purchased a library of

MGM movies, one of which was *The Wizard of Oz*. In an offbeat attempt at cross-promotion, WCW promoters had decided to name some of their wrestlers after characters in MGM movies. This is how Nash became known as Oz.

As Oz, Nash dyed his hair silver and wore green tights and a rubber mask. His manager, Kevin Sullivan, was called the Wizard. When Oz made his first appearance at SuperBrawl I on May 19, 1991, he was accompanied by the Wizard, Dorothy, Toto, the Tin Man, the Scarecrow, and the Cowardly Lion. Nash wondered, "Am I a wrestler or something out of a comic book?" The answer, of course, was that he was both.

With the classic film *The Wizard of Oz* as inspiration, Kevin followed his own "yellow brick road" to success and stardom.

The Dark Days in WCW

Although the people in the crowd couldn't believe what they were watching, Oz proved that he was no joke by pinning Tim Parker in twenty-six seconds. Oz had invented a move called the helicopter slam, in which he spun his opponent over his head for several seconds, then slammed him to the mat. Nonetheless, Oz wasn't ready for prime time. At the Great American Bash on July 4, 1991, Oz lost quickly to Ron Simmons, one of the top singles wrestlers in the federation and a future WCW world champion.

Kevin Nash needed training and experience more than he needed a gimmick. Although he wanted people to take him seriously, WCW promoters started using Oz on fewer and fewer cards. The fans booed him relentlessly. They mocked his outfit and his name. Eventually, WCW promoters exchanged one gimmick for another, and Oz became Vinnie Vegas, a casino bouncer. At first, Vinnie Vegas looked good. On January 21, 1992, he pinned former world champion Tommy Rich in less than a minute. Manager Harley Race made him part of his Half Ton of Holy Hell stable, along with Big Van Vader and Mr. Hughes. But when Vader won the world heavyweight title on July 12, 1992, Race started paying more attention to Vader than his other men.

The Dark Days in WCW

Changes in name and management did nothing to help Nash's career. He joined Diamond Dallas Page's Diamond Mine stable and teamed with Page for a while, but he made little progress. As a singles wrestler, Vegas lost to Erik Watts and 2 Cold Scorpio—men barely half his weight. At Halloween Havoc '92, Vegas and Page lost to Watts and Hammer in a tag team match. Some of his matches didn't even have anything to do with pro wrestling. At Clash of the Champions XXII on January 13, 1993, Vegas beat Tony Atlas in an arm wrestling match.

Finally, in early 1993, Nash's contract with WCW expired. He was ready for a change.

4 The Diesel Train

On May 17, 1993, Shawn Michaels lost the World Wrestling Federation intercontinental championship to Marty Jannetty. The loss incensed Michaels. Jannetty was his former tag team partner and had enlisted wrestler Curt Hennig to help him win and defend the belt. Michaels, one of the most talented wrestlers in the world, would do anything to win and realized that he had to even the sides with Jannetty.

The Diesel Train

Michaels learned through several sources that Kevin Nash's contract with WCW had expired. Michaels called Nash and asked him, "Do you want to be my bodyguard?" Actually, Nash wanted to wrestle, but he would do anything to get away from WCW. He agreed to join Michaels in the WWF.

Michaels introduced Nash as his bodyguard on June 6, 1993, in Albany, New York. Jannetty was Michaels's opponent that night, and for the first several minutes of the match, Nash stood in front of Michaels and protected him from Jannetty. When the action started and Jannetty was on the verge of victory, Nash tripped Jannetty, enabling Michaels to score the pin and regain the title. Already, Nash was paying dividends for his new boss.

Nash changed his ring name to Diesel and helped Michaels defend the title against Crush at the King of the Ring pay-per-view match one week later. At SummerSlam '93, Diesel's interference again was key as Michaels defeated Hennig by countout. Diesel gained a reputation as a ruthless bodyguard who would do anything to help his man win. Not only was he physically imposing, he was also violent and strong, and he totally disregarded the rules. If Michaels needed help, Nash helped him.

Michaels was stripped of the title on September 27, 1993, for failing to meet contractual obligations. Soon after, Michaels left

The Diesel Train

the WWF, leaving Diesel with nothing to do but return to the ring as a wrestler. At first, it seemed that Diesel was a much better bodyguard than a wrestler. He lost most of his matches. At the 1993 Survivor Series, he teamed with Irwin R. Schyster, Rick Martel, and Adam Bomb and lost to Marty Jannetty, Razor Ramon, the Kid, and Randy Savage.

Michaels eventually settled his differences with the WWF and returned to the ring. But Diesel wasn't sure that he wanted to return to his duties as a bodyguard. He wanted to wrestle. After all, that was his plan when he had first moved to Atlanta and had started training at the Power Plant. Nonetheless, the truth couldn't be ignored.

Nash and the Outsiders often battled Lex Luger, one of WCW's hottest superstars.

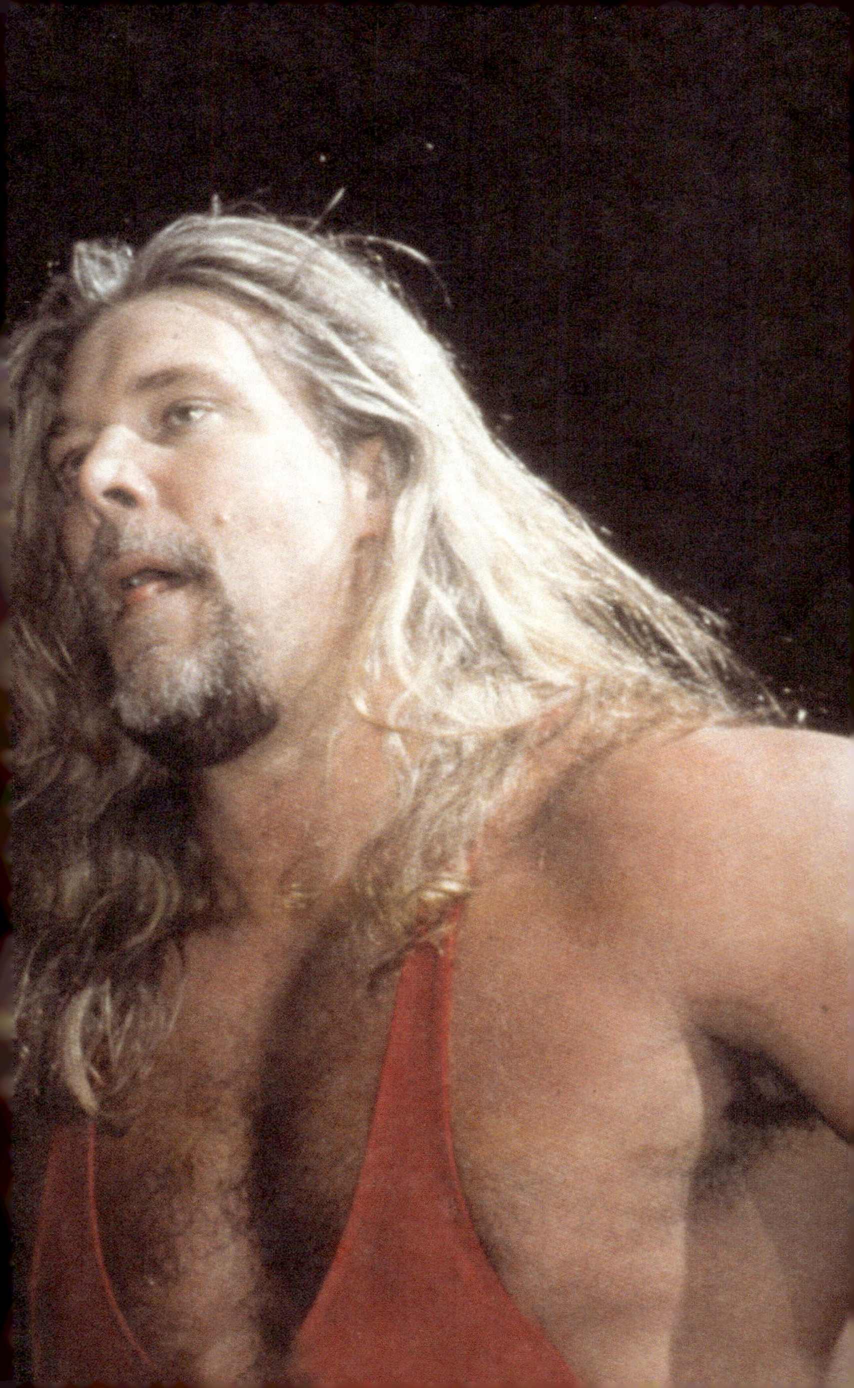

Everything changed at the Royal Rumble on January 22, 1994, in Providence, Rhode Island. The Royal Rumble—a battle royal in which the wrestlers enter the ring one at a time every two minutes until all thirty wrestlers have entered—is one of the most important events on the WWF's annual schedule. The only way to eliminate a wrestler is by dumping him over the top rope and onto the arena floor. The last person remaining is the winner, and the winner receives a match against the WWF world champion on the show *WrestleMania*.

Diesel was spectacular in the Royal Rumble. He eliminated Bart Gunn, Scott Steiner, Owen Hart, Kwang, Bob

The Diesel Train

Backlund, Billy Gunn, and Virgil before three men combined to eliminate him. Although he didn't win the Royal Rumble, Diesel was the star of the show. He had proven just how imposing he could be.

Diesel set his sights on the intercontinental title (also called the I-C) held by Razor Ramon. Ramon, who beat Michaels in a ladder match on *WrestleMania X*, squared off against Diesel on April 13, 1994, at War Memorial Auditorium in Rochester, New York. Ramon had held the intercontinental championship title for seven months, and there was no reason to believe that a neophyte like Diesel would have any chance against him.

That night, the War Memorial Auditorium was packed for the WWF television taping. Earlier, Ramon had beaten Diesel by disqualification when Michaels interfered. Diesel was seven feet tall, but Ramon was six feet eight inches and weighed 290 pounds, so he was not at all intimidated by his opponent's size. When the bell rang, Ramon went right after Diesel and brawled with his slightly larger rival.

However, the Michaels factor couldn't be ignored. Ramon was convinced that Michaels would eventually interfere, and he kept on looking over his shoulder. When Michaels started taunting Ramon, the champion turned his attention away from Diesel. It was the worst mistake he

The Diesel Train

could have made. Michaels climbed into the ring, and Ramon went after him. Michaels went back outside the ring, and Ramon continued the chase. Diesel snuck out after Ramon, and when Ramon turned around, Diesel kicked him in the face. Both men got back into the ring. Diesel delivered a jackknife power-bomb. Ramon crumpled to the mat. Diesel dropped on top of Ramon and scored the pin. Diesel was the new I-C champion.

The Diesel train was on the move.

Having made his entrance as Diesel the bodyguard at the 1993 King of the Ring, Diesel made himself known as a force to be reckoned with at the 1994 King of the Ring. His opponent was WWF

Nash battled Bret "the Hitman" Hart, a five-time WWF heavyweight champion and half of the legendary tag team the Hart Foundation.

world champion Bret Hart, one of the finest all-around wrestlers in the world. It was a classic battle of size and strength versus skill. In this case, size and strength dominated. Diesel tossed Hart around the ring, whipped him into the ropes, and floored the champ with an elbow to the stomach. Hart dropped to the mat, and Diesel went in for the pin. But when Jim

The Diesel Train

Neidhart interfered and clotheslined Diesel, the referee disqualified Hart. Diesel had won the match, but because titles don't change hands on disqualifications (unless special rules are stipulated), Hart was still champion. Regardless, anybody who had watched the match couldn't deny that Diesel was the better wrestler.

Having won the intercontinental title and taken the world champion to the brink, Diesel was no longer content with being Shawn Michaels's bodyguard. Diesel and Michaels formed a successful tag team, while denying rumors that there were differences between them. On August 28, 1994, Diesel and Michaels battled WWF world tag team champions the

Headshrinkers in Indianapolis, Indiana. Late in the match, Diesel avoided Samu's pin attempt and then pinned Samu. Not only were Diesel and Michaels world tag team champions, but Diesel had two titles.

The next night, at SummerSlam '94, Diesel had Michaels in his corner for his match against Razor Ramon. Ramon had former NFL player Walter Payton in his corner. Michaels interfered, and Diesel held Ramon. Michaels attempted his superkick. When Ramon ducked, Michaels kicked Diesel in the chin. Diesel dropped to the mat. Ramon swooped in and scored the pin. Ramon was the new intercontinental champion, and Diesel was thoroughly incensed.

The Diesel Train

Although rumors were flying about the squabbling between Diesel and Michaels, the tag team champions continued to defend the belts. But at the 1994 Survivor Series, Diesel and Michaels teamed with Neidhart, Owen Hart, and Jeff Jarrett against Ramon, the Kid, Davey Boy Smith, Sionne, and Fatu. Diesel eliminated Fatu, the Kid, and Sionne. Ramon was the only man left on the other team. Diesel held Ramon as Michaels prepared for a superkick. Again, Ramon ducked, and Michaels struck Diesel in the face.

Diesel got up, stormed after Michaels, and chased him back to the locker room, where he and Michaels shouted at each other for several minutes.

The team of Diesel and Michaels was history. The next night, the world tag team belts were declared vacant, meaning that nobody was champion.

However, as had been the case when his WCW contract expired, Diesel found a way to turn a seemingly bad situation into something good.

The World Champion

Although Shawn Michaels would go on to become one of the most popular wrestlers in the world, in 1994, he was a bad guy—meaning that anybody who opposed him was a good guy. For the first time in his WWF career, Diesel was a fan favorite, and he was about to make history.

On November 26, 1994, at Madison Square Garden in New York, less than eight

In only eight months, Nash won the most prestigious titles in the WWF: the intercontinental, the world tag team, and the world heavyweight titles.

The World Champion

months after he won the intercontinental title, Diesel stepped into the ring against WWF world champion Bob Backlund. Backlund was a crafty wrestler, but he was no match for Diesel. When the bell rang, Diesel stepped into the ring and booted Backlund in the stomach. Then he lifted Backlund and jackknife power-bombed him to the mat. Diesel swooped in for the pin. The referee made the three count. The match lasted only eight seconds. Diesel was WWF world heavyweight champion.

It was a remarkable accomplishment. In under eight months, Diesel had won the three most important titles in the WWF: the intercontinental, world tag team, and world heavyweight titles.

Kevin Nash

The man who had been such a loser in WCW was now wrestling's biggest winner.

Diesel was also the WWF's biggest moving target. At the 1995 Royal Rumble, a match between Diesel and Bret Hart ended because Michaels, Owen Hart, Jeff Jarrett, Bob Backlund, and the Roadie interfered. Michaels won the Royal Rumble and a match against Diesel on *WrestleMania XI*, but Diesel got lucky. At that match, Michaels had Diesel covered for a pin for ten seconds, but referee Dave Hebner had twisted his ankle while trying to stop Sid Vicious from interfering on Michaels's behalf. When Hebner finally started counting, Diesel kicked out. Seconds later, Diesel used his jackknife to pin the Heartbreak Kid.

The World Champion

Michaels blamed Vicious for the loss, so Vicious attacked him the following night on *Monday Night Raw*. Diesel surprised everyone by saving Michaels from the attack, but Michaels had to be taken to the hospital for treatment.

"I owe Shawn a lot," Diesel said. "I don't know if what happened tonight means we're friends or not. I knew Sid was bad news."

The truth of the matter was that he was worse news than Diesel had ever imagined. At In Your House I, on May 14, 1995, Diesel battled Vicious in the main event. Late in the match, Vicious power-bombed Diesel to the canvas, then covered Diesel for the pin. Incredibly, Diesel kicked out and went on to win the match by disqualification when Tatanka interfered. Diesel suffered an injured right elbow in the match and had to undergo surgery to remove bone chips.

Diesel and Vicious met again at In Your House II, on July 23, 1995. It was a lumberjack match, in which friends and foes of both wrestlers surround the ring and prevent the wrestlers from escaping. These wrestlers, however, spent most of the time beating up Diesel and Vicious. Mabel, a 568-pound monster, legdropped Diesel on the arena floor. Fortunately for Diesel, Michaels prevented Vicious from making the pin. Diesel booted Vicious in the chin and then pinned his arch rival. At

The World Champion

SummerSlam on August 27, 1995, Diesel needed less than ten minutes to pin Mabel.

As the year wore on, Diesel not only established himself as a formidable WWF world champion, but also as an impressive tag team wrestler with Shawn Michaels. At In Your House III, on September 24, Diesel and Michaels took on world tag team champions Yokozuna and Davey Boy Smith. Smith was filling in for the injured Owen Hart, but Hart came to the ring late in the match. Diesel pinned Hart and apparently won the world tag team championship. But a day later, WWF commissioner Gorilla Monsoon reversed the decision and gave the belts back to Yokozuna and Hart.

Diesel ran into another Hart—Bret—at In Your House IV on October 22, 1995. That night, Diesel defended his title against Davey Boy Smith in Winnipeg, Manitoba. With Diesel hobbled and apparently on the verge of defeat, TV commentator/wrestler Bret Hart stormed into the ring and attacked Davey Boy. Diesel was disqualified. Angry over what had happened, Diesel went after Bret. The two engaged in a slugfest, and afterward Diesel declared, "Bret had no right to get involved."

> "Bret had no right to get involved."
> -Diesel said regarding the In Your House IV match

The result was a match between the current world champion Diesel and the

The World Champion

former world champion Bret Hart at the Survivor Series on November 19, 1995, in Landover, Maryland. Both men were fan favorites, so the fans didn't know whom to root for. It was a sensational match, and both men scored several near-pinfalls. Late in the match, Hart fell to the arena floor. When he tried to return to the ring, Diesel kicked him through a table. Hart crawled back into the ring, seemingly badly injured. Diesel got ready to deliver his jackknife power-bomb. Diesel started to lift Hart, but Bret grabbed Diesel's legs, dragged him to the mat, and scored the pin. Hart was the new WWF world champion, and Diesel wasn't happy. He jackknifed Hart twice onto the canvas, then

Kevin Nash

attacked three referees. The crowd booed in disbelief. Suddenly, Diesel was a rule-breaker again.

The year ended with Diesel taking out his frustration by power-bombing Owen Hart several times at In Your House V, on December 17, 1995. Diesel was ranked number one in *Pro Wrestling Illustrated* magazine's annual ranking of the top 300 wrestlers in the world. Diesel would also be named Wrestler of the Year by *PWI*'s readers, and his match against Shawn Michaels on *WrestleMania* would be named Match of the Year. His world title reign, which lasted one week short of a year, had proven to the world that Diesel was an outstanding wrestler.

The World Champion

But 1996 would be a year of change for Diesel. He started teaming with Razor Ramon and feuded with the Undertaker, who had been named top contender to the world title. Diesel appeared to be ready to regain the belt from Bret Hart in a steel cage at In Your House VI on February 18, 1996, when the Undertaker broke through the ring and prevented Diesel from walking out the cage door (in a cage match, a wrestler can win by pinning his opponent, climbing over the top of the cage, or exiting through the cage door).

But that cage door wasn't the only thing Diesel planned on walking out of. In March, Diesel announced that he would leave the WWF after his contract expired on June 6. A few months later, Razor Ramon signed with WCW, reverted to his real name, Scott Hall, and told WCW senior vice president Eric Bischoff that he was bringing in two more wrestlers. Would Diesel be one of them?

"We're taking over!" Hall proclaimed.

The "we" turned out to be Hall and Diesel. A day after his contract expired, Diesel returned to WCW as Kevin Nash. As the Outsiders, Nash and Hall were a team that would change the course of wrestling history.

The New World Order

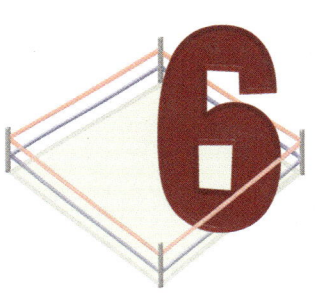

Scott Hall and Kevin Nash didn't wrestle at WCW's Great American Bash on June 16, 1996, but they made a greater impact than the wrestlers there. First, they told Eric Bischoff that they and a mystery partner wanted to wrestle WCW's three best wrestlers. Then, when Bischoff made the mistake of telling them that they'd have to wait until after the Bash to find out the names of their opponents, Nash and Hall slammed him on the stage.

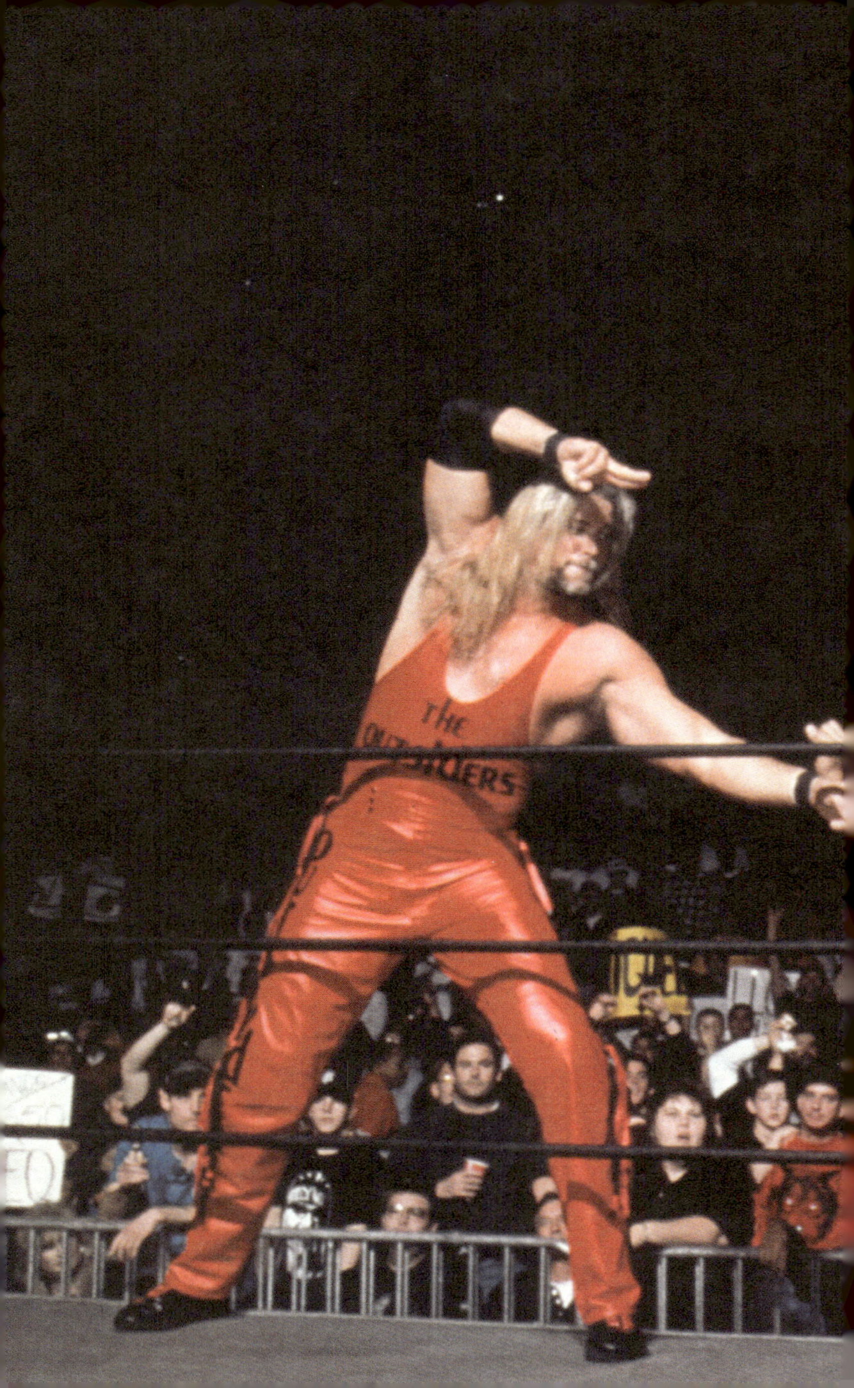
THE

The New World Order had one purpose: to wreak havoc on World Championship Wrestling. They weren't above using questionable tactics to accomplish this task.

Their three opponents at Bash at the Beach, on July 7, 1996, were to be Sting, Lex Luger, and Randy Savage, but most fans were more interested in finding out the name of the Outsiders' mystery partner. Nash and Hall started the match without their mystery partner. When Luger got hurt and had to be taken away on a stretcher, Hulk Hogan appeared on the runway. Hogan, the former WWF world champion, was the most successful and popular wrestler in the world.

Most people assumed that he was there to help Savage and Sting. But when Hogan stepped into the ring, his true intentions became clear. He legdropped Savage and high-fived Nash and Hall.

The New World Order

The third Outsider was Hogan. The NWO—the New World Order—was born. Its purpose: to wreak havoc on WCW.

The NWO was ruthless. Hall, Nash, and Hogan attacked anyone who got in their way. They attacked several opponents with baseball bats. On August 10, 1996, Hall and Nash helped Hogan beat the Giant for the WCW world heavyweight title. Every episode of WCW's *Nitro* television show featured the NWO injuring opponents, taking over the broadcast booth, and showing shameless disregard for the rules. Nash and Hall laughed when their interference cost Luger the WCW TV title. They recruited several wrestlers into the NWO, including the Giant, Ted DiBiase, and Syxx. At Halloween

Nash poses with Hulk Hogan, one of the most popular wrestlers in the world.

The New World Order

Havoc, on October 27, 1996, Nash and Hall stole Colonel Robert Parker's cane and used it to beat Parker's team, Harlem Heat, for the WCW world tag team title.

Nash and Hall had attitude. Nash wore his beard in a goatee and sported leather vests. He was big, he had an intense gaze, and he looked tough. He called himself Big Sexy. Hall wore his hair slicked back and had a toothpick hanging out of his mouth. He was the Bad Guy. Together, they meant trouble. They were unpredictable, ruthless, and dangerous. When Bischoff joined the group, the New World Order was in position to take over WCW. In fact, the NWO even demanded that it get its own heavyweight championship, the NWO world heavyweight title. However, that request was denied.

The irony of the situation was that although the NWO had been formed to destroy WCW, it was actually helping the WWF. Prior to the emergence of the NWO, WCW was second to the WWF in attendance, prestige, and Monday night TV ratings. Thanks to the interest generated by the NWO, *Nitro* started dominating *Raw* in the Monday night ratings.

The NWO had its own pay-per-view event, Souled Out, on January 25, 1997, and, as would be expected, the NWO dictated the rules. Nash and Hall defended the tag team championship against Rick and Scott Steiner. The NWO had its own

The New World Order

referee for the match, Nick Patrick, but he was knocked out during a scuffle and was replaced by WCW referee Randy Anderson. When Scott Steiner pinned Hall, Anderson made the pin. The Steiners appeared to be the new world tag team champions, but the decision was reversed by Bischoff because the wrong referee had made the count. Nash and Hall were still champions. Nobody could argue with Bischoff's ruling. After all, he was still senior vice president of WCW.

Several wrestlers, including Diamond Dallas Page and Roddy Piper, made destroying the NWO their top priority. At Uncensored, Team NWO, consisting of Nash, Hall, Hulk Hogan, and Randy Savage,

Nash puts the hurt on Randy Savage during a match.

The New World Order

wrestled in a three-team match. If Team NWO won, it would have the right to demand shots at any WCW title whenever it pleased. The opposition was Team WCW (the Giant, Lex Luger, and Rick and Scott Steiner), and Team Piper (Piper, Jeff Jarrett, Chris Benoit, and Steve McMichael). In Team NWO's corner was bad boy basketball star Dennis Rodman. Rodman interfered, and Team NWO won.

Of course, as with any clique populated by egotistical individuals, internal dissent is always a potential problem. Predictably, the members of the NWO started squabbling with each other. At Spring Stampede '97, a match between Nash and Rick Steiner was declared a no-contest when referee Nick Patrick walked out, refusing to count Nash's attempted pin of Steiner. Ted DiBiase, who had become very religious, even urged his teammates to have mercy on their opponents. The NWO responded by firing DiBiase and feuding with Piper and Ric Flair. However, at Slamboree '97, Flair, Piper, and Kevin Greene combined to beat Hall, Nash, and Syxx. Hall and Nash continued to dominate the WCW world tag team title and they beat Flair and Piper at the Great American Bash on June 15, 1997. The NWO added another member when Curt Hennig defected from his team at Fall Brawl on September 14, 1997. Hennig was a former NWA world champion.

The New World Order

On September 19, 1997, Nash suffered torn ligaments in his right knee while wrestling in Seattle, Washington. He was sidelined for three months. Syxx replaced Nash in tag team title defenses, and on October 13, 1997, Syxx and Hall lost the belts to Rick and Scott Steiner.

Nash returned in November and began a feud with former NWO member the Giant over who was the real giant in WCW. Nash disguised himself as Sting and attacked the Giant with a baseball bat at World War III on November 23, 1997. On January 12, 1998, Hall and Nash regained the tag belts from the Steiners. In a showdown at Souled Out on January 24, 1998, Nash tossed hot coffee in the Giant's face

Nash was an aggressive force against his opponents, often taunting them at matches.

and power-bombed the Giant, who then suffered a concussion.

Hall and Nash lost the belts to the Steiners on February 9, regained them on February 22, and lost them again to the Giant and Sting on May 17, 1998. In the meantime, Nash and Hall had other things to worry about: serious internal turmoil in the NWO. When Bischoff fired Syxx, one of

The New World Order

Nash's best friends, Hogan stated publicly that Syxx wasn't good enough for the NWO. The comment incensed Nash, who got even angrier when, on *Nitro*, Hogan interfered in his match against WCW world champion Sting (who had won the belt from Hogan).

With Hogan and Nash at odds and Hall stuck in the middle, the NWO couldn't survive much longer. Something had to give.

Would the NWO cease to exist?

Not by a long shot.

Instead of one NWO, there was about to be two.

7 One Becomes Two Becomes One

The New World Order should have known it was courting disaster when Hulk Hogan and Kevin Nash teamed up at Spring Stampede on April 19, 1998. Their opponents were Roddy Piper and the Giant, but their real foes were each other.

Late in the match, Hogan accidentally struck Nash in the stomach with a baseball bat. Hogan won the match for his team by pinning Piper, but Nash refused to join in on

One Becomes Two Becomes One

the celebration. Hogan responded by slugging Nash with the bat.

One night later at *Nitro*, Nash interfered in Hogan's match against new WCW world champion Randy Savage. Nash climbed into the ring and power-bombed Hogan.

"I'm through with Hogan," Nash said.

The NWO split into two: NWO Wolfpac, with Nash as the leader, and NWO Hollywood, with Hogan as the leader. But who would Hall side with, his friend, or Hogan and Bischoff?

"Me and Kev are tighter than ever," Hall said. "I'm NWO for life."

A week later, at Slamboree '98, Hall and Nash defended the world tag team title

The **NWO** split into two factions: **NWO** Wolfpac, with Nash as the leader, and **NWO** Hollywood, with Hogan as chief.

One Becomes Two Becomes One

against Sting and the Giant. Nash was about to pin the Giant when Hall hit Nash over the head with a championship belt, then rolled the Giant on top of Nash. The referee counted the pin. Hall and Nash were no longer the world tag team champions. Hall had gone Hollywood.

The Wolfpac consisted of Nash, Luger, Savage, Sting, Hennig, and Konnan. Hollywood consisted of Hogan, Hall, and Dusty Rhodes. The fans were on the side of the Wolfpac.

However, Hall and Nash were reluctant to battle each other. They weren't ready to toss aside their friendship just yet. Nash tried to help Hall in a title match against Hogan, but Hall didn't want any help.

Kevin Nash

Hall attacked Nash, and then Nash attacked Hall on *Nitro*, which resulted in a brawl between the two NWO factions. Now Hall and Nash were bitter enemies. At Road Wild on August 8, 1998, Nash and Hall slugged it out after they had both been eliminated from a battle royal.

During the fall of 1998, Hall and Stevie Ray unleashed a brutal attack on Nash. Weeks later, the Wolfpac destroyed NWO Hollywood's limousine. Then, Hall attacked Nash in a bar. The two men had car chases through city streets. It has been said that former friends make the most bitter enemies, and Hall and Nash were proving that adage true. They battled in the ring at Halloween Havoc on October 25, 1998.

Nash stunned Hall with two power-bombs, but walked away from the ring without attempting a pin and was counted out. One night later on *Nitro*, Hall and the Giant attacked Nash.

Nash, who had been WWF world champion but never the WCW champion, won a battle royal in which the prize was a shot at world champion Bill Goldberg at Starrcade '98. Starrcade, WCW's most important pay-per-view event of the year, was held on December 27 in Washington, D.C. Goldberg was about to pin Nash when Disco Inferno, who wanted to join the Wolfpac, interfered. Goldberg turned his attention away from Nash and threw Inferno out of the ring. Bam Bam Bigelow

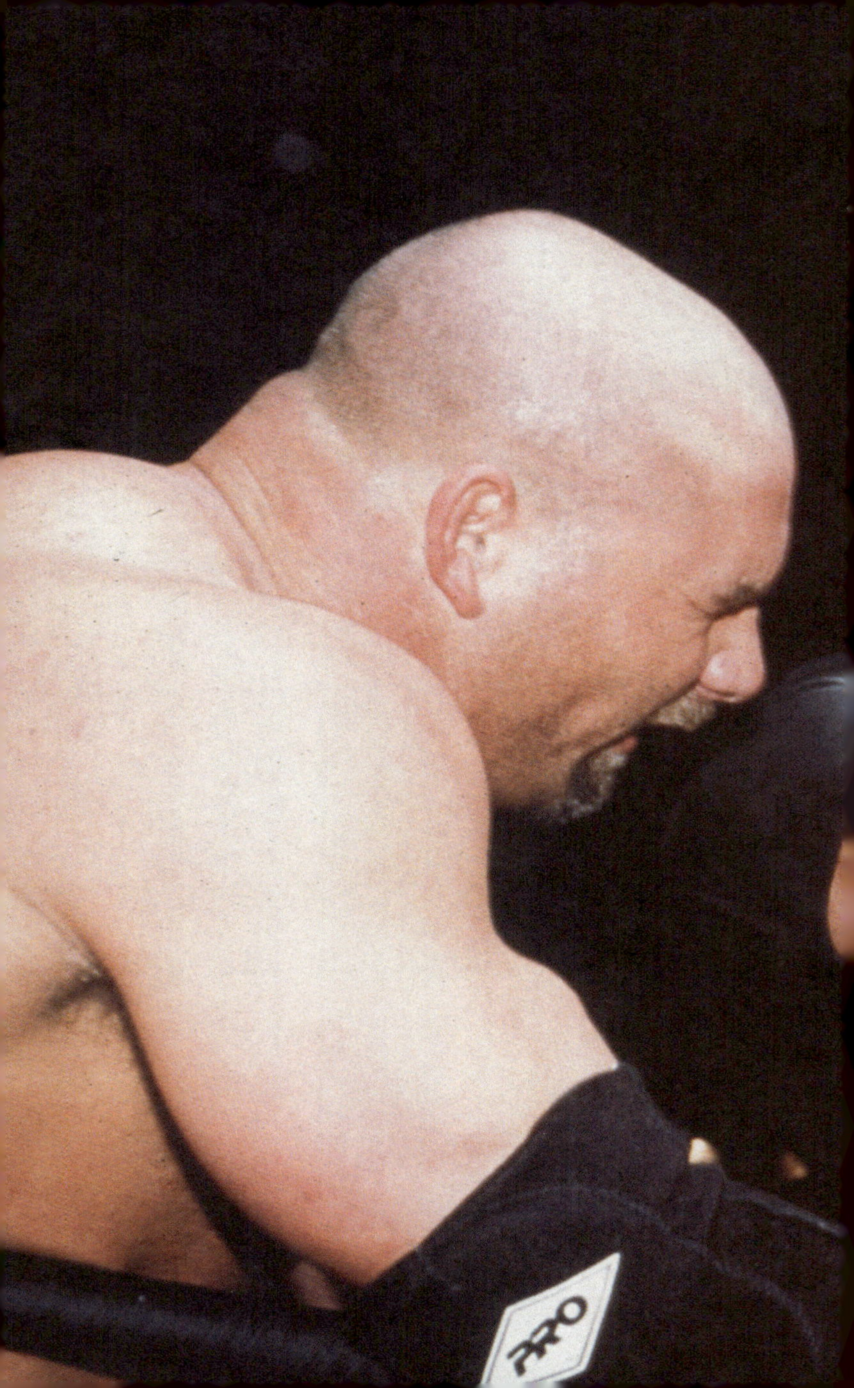
PRO

Goldberg and Nash battled often throughout their careers.

Kevin Nash

tried to interfere, but Goldberg got rid of him, too.

Then Hall, dressed as a security guard, walked to the ring. The fans had no doubt that he was there to help Goldberg. But, as it turned out, the fans were wrong. Hall climbed into the ring and stunned Goldberg with an electric cattle prod. Goldberg fell to the mat, convulsing in pain. Nash got up and pounced on top of Goldberg. The referee made the three-count. Nash was WCW world champion.

Nash and Hall celebrated in the ring. The Outsiders had reunited in stunning fashion. But the real stunner was yet to come. On January 4, 1999, Nash allowed Hogan to pin him for the world title. Then

One Becomes Two Becomes One

he got up and hugged Hall, Hogan, and Scott Steiner. The days of two NWOs were over. The NWO was back with a vengeance.

Hogan lost the world title to Ric Flair in mid-March, but Nash got it back for the NWO when he beat long-time NWO foe Diamond Dallas Page at Slamboree on May 9, 1999. Randy Savage's interference nearly cost Nash the match, and Nash responded by filling Savage's limousine with raw sewage.

Nash appeared on *The Tonight Show with Jay Leno* and challenged Bret Hart to a match. He even put up $250,000 out of his own pocket. The match never happened because Bret's brother, Owen, died after a WWF match.

Nash and Sting went up against Savage and Sid Vicious at Bash at the Beach on July 11, 1999. Every wrestler in the ring, including Sting, was eligible to beat Nash for the world title. Sting double-crossed Nash by flooring him with a Stinger splash. Afterward, Savage scored the pin. Nash lost the world title because of his partner's duplicity.

> "If you want to know Sting's real colors, look at his back: It's yellow."
> -Nash said of Sting's dishonest victory

"Belts come and go," Nash said. "What bothers me more than losing the belt is how sneaky Sting has become. Forget the red and black, forget the black and white. If you want to know Sting's real colors, look at his back: It's yellow. Sting had a chance to prove that he was on my side tonight and he didn't do it. That's all I need to know."

One night later on *Nitro*, Nash helped Hogan win the title from Savage, and demanded a shot against his NWO partner. Hogan was angry at Nash for demanding a title shot and accused him of not being a team player. Nash responded that he had laid down for Hogan in January and wanted a chance to regain the title he had unselfishly given up. Hogan and Nash battled at Road Wild on August 14, 1999, in Sturgis, North Dakota. The stipulation of the match was that the loser had to retire.

Nash failed to become three-time **WCW** world champion and was forced into retirement, but he would be back—with a vengeance.

One Becomes Two Becomes One

Nash seemed to be on the verge of victory when he rocked Hogan with a power-bomb and covered him for the pin. Hogan kicked out just in time, then went on to win the match by pinfall. Nash had not only failed in his attempt to become three-time WCW world champion, but he had been forced into retirement.

"I'll be back," Nash declared.

But how? And when?

8 Return to Superstardom

"When" turned out to be less than two months later on *Nitro*, on October 4, 1999. "How" turned out to be as an audience member with Scott Hall sitting beside him.

Two weeks later, Nash and Hall taunted Goldberg from their ringside seats and were escorted out of the arena. At Halloween Havoc on October 24, Nash and Hall attacked Goldberg as he was making his entrance for a match against Sid Vicious.

Nash watches a match with the NWO.

Goldberg was dead set on revenge. The next night on *Nitro*, Goldberg speared both Hall and Nash. However, Hall and Nash got in the last shot. Their interference cost Goldberg the U.S. title in a match against Bret Hart.

A few weeks later, Nash was special referee in a four-way match for the U.S. title involving Goldberg, Hart, Vicious, and

Hall. Nash bashed Hart with a baseball bat and helped Hall win the title. Now Nash was ready for his return to the ring.

On November 15, Nash, dressed up as Sid Vicious, taunted Vicious. Vicious responded by challenging Nash to a match.

"I'm retired," Nash said.

But the powers that be, who were running the show in WCW, lifted Nash's retirement. Nash wrestled Vicious in a street fight, but Hall and Goldberg interfered, resulting in a brawl. Hall and Nash versus Goldberg and Vicious became a regular event on *Nitro*. One night, Hall and Nash battled Goldberg and Vicious and Benoit and Hart in a three-way cage

It's hard to tell who has the upper hand in this body slam as Goldberg and Nash fly through the air at a match-turned-brawl.

match. This chaotic brawl ended with Jeff Jarrett joining the Outsiders in a violent attack on all four opponents.

Meanwhile, Goldberg and Hart had won the WCW world tag team title, and the Outsiders wanted the belts back. The teams clashed on *Nitro* on December 13, and Nash pinned Hart to win the championship.

At Starrcade, Nash battled Vicious in a match in which the only way to win was by power-bombing and pinning your opponent. Nash never power-bombed Vicious, but he convinced the referee that he had and won the match. A night later on *Nitro*, a reunion took place when Nash and Hall helped Bret Hart beat Goldberg. At the end of the night, Nash announced that the band was back together: Nash, Hall, Jarrett, and Hart. The new NWO.

The new NWO was like the original one; together, they wreaked havoc on WCW. When the Outsiders were stripped of the tag team belts because Hall didn't show up for a match on time, members of the NWO attacked WCW officials, vandalized Sid

Nash, attired in his Outsiders' costume, administers a brutal chopping kick to an opponent.

Vicious's car, and used baseball bats to help Hart and Jarrett win their matches. At Souled Out 2000, Nash battled Terry Funk to determine who would be commissioner of WCW. Nash jackknifed Funk through three chairs and scored the pin. The next night, Nash exercised his power as commissioner to return the U.S. title to Jeff Jarrett, who had lost the belt to Benoit at Souled Out.

Nash was wilder than ever. He placed a $15,000 bounty on Funk's head. He stripped Sid Vicious of the WCW world title. When he injured his ankle, Nash named Jarrett acting commissioner, but Nash returned to the job, accusing Jarrett of making too many mistakes. Jarrett turned against Nash. And then things changed in WCW.

On *Nitro*, on April 10, Eric Bischoff and Vince Russo of WCW announced that the time had come to give the federation's younger stars a chance. This meant that Nash, Hall, Flair, Hogan, Sting, Luger, and Diamond Dallas Page were being pushed aside, and they didn't like that at all.

Return to Superstardom

Nash's first order of business in the feud between the New Blood (the young stars) and the Millionaires' Club (the established stars) was a feud with former WCW heavyweight champion Mike Awesome. Nash jackknifed Awesome through a table and attacked both Awesome and Billy Kidman on *Nitro* on April 24, 2000. Nash became Flair's ally. Russo, along with Jarrett and David Flair (Ric's son), became Nash's arch enemy.

Nash got another shot at the WCW world title in a three-way match involving Jarrett and Scott Steiner at Thunder on May 24. Steiner prevented Russo from interfering, and Nash jackknifed Jarrett to win the world title. Five days later on

Nitro, Nash handed the world title to Ric Flair simply because he felt Flair deserved it. That marked the second time in Nash's career that he had willingly sacrificed the world title.

The world title was changing hands almost weekly, and when Jarrett won the world title, Nash received a shot against him at the Great American Bash. The Filthy Animals, including Kidman, attacked Nash. Then Goldberg speared Nash, enabling Jarrett to score the pin.

Goldberg and Nash feuded intensely. At Bash at the Beach on July 9, 2000, Scott Steiner attacked Nash, then Goldberg speared and jackhammered Nash to win the match. Afterward, Steiner again

Nash was aggressive inside and outside of the ring, going so far as to place a $15,000 bounty on Terry Funk.

attacked Nash. The loss meant that Scott Hall was out of WCW and that Nash had a new enemy: Scott Steiner. At New Blood Rising on August 13, Nash beat Steiner to become the number one contender to the world title.

Each week brought new surprises and changes on *Nitro*. On August 28, Nash came to the arena with Scott Steiner,

Jeff Jarrett, and Vince Russo, and declared that he would become the next WCW world champion. He was given a match against world champion Booker T, and he beat him to become world champion again. Nash defended the title against Booker T in a cage match at Fall Brawl on September 17 and lost after missing with a jackknife. Again, the world title changed hands. Nash got a chance to regain the title on *Nitro* on November 6, but interference by Shawn Stasiak enabled Booker T to keep the belt.

No matter where he goes, and no matter who he wrestles, Kevin Nash will always make headlines. Nash shocked the wrestling world in late November 2000

Kevin Nash parlayed his successful wrestling career into a lucrative television career.

when he befriended former NWO foe Diamond Dallas Page. At the Mayhem pay-per-view on November 26, Nash and Page beat Chuck Palumbo and Shawn Stasiak for the world title, but they lost the belts the next night on *Nitro*.

Who knows how many title victories and surprises are in Nash's future. Certainly, his career has been one big surprise after another. From his early struggles as Master Blaster Steel, to his stunning victories as Diesel in the WWF, to his role in the emergence of the New World Order as a wrestling power, Nash has been front and center in the wrestling world. He has appeared on such television shows as *Politically*

Incorrect, *The Tonight Show with Jay Leno*, *Live with Regis and Kathy Lee*, *Sabrina: The Teenage Witch*, and *The Love Boat*. He is featured in his own comic book, called *Nash*, about a futuristic hero who battles a villain named Cyrus Storm in the year 2023.

This is one train that has not nearly reached its last stop.

Glossary

assembly line Arrangement of workers, machines, and equipment in which the product being assembled passes from operation to operation until completed.

card List of matches on a wrestling show.

clothesline Offensive move in which the attacking wrestler sticks out his arm and uses it to strike the victim in the neck.

Glossary

The clothesline is often executed by whipping the opponent into the ropes, then striking him in the neck on the rebound.

countout A wrestler is counted out if he is out of the ring for twenty seconds or more. When the wrestler leaves the ring, the referee begins his count at one. If the wrestler is counted out, he is disqualified.

disqualification In wrestling, a wrestler can lose by disqualification if he uses a foreign object, refuses to obey the referee's orders, breaks the rules repeatedly, is counted out of the ring, or if another person interferes on his behalf.

Except in the event of a double disqualification—in which both wrestlers lose—the victory is awarded to his opponent. In most championship matches, the belt does not change hands on a disqualification, only on a pin or submission.

feud Series of matches between two wrestlers or two tag teams. Many times, one wrestler will bad-mouth the other wrestler or will sneak attack the wrestler.

jackknife power-bomb Offensive wrestling maneuver in which the attacker lifts his opponent waist-high, then drives him shoulder-first into the mat.

Glossary

kick out To kick out of a hold.

legdrop Offensive maneuver, used most frequently by Hulk Hogan, in which the attacker drops his body leg-first onto his opponent's prone body.

no-contest Outcome in a wrestling match in which a winner isn't declared. This should not be confused with a double-disqualification, in which both sides lose.

pin When either both shoulders or both shoulder blades are held in contact with the mat for three continuous seconds. A pin ends a match.

power-bomb To lift and drop an opponent to the mat while holding onto him.

promoter The person responsible for hiring and contracting the wrestlers for a card or federation. The promoter is also responsible for deciding the matchups for a card.

spear To crouch, run at your opponent, and slam him.

submission hold Move that makes an opponent give up without being pinned.

superkick Offensive move, popularized by Shawn Michaels, in which the attacker kicks his leg high in the air and strikes his opponent in the chin with the bottom of his foot.

Sweet Sixteen The round of sixteen teams in the NCAA basketball tournament.

For More Information

Magazines

Pro Wrestling Illustrated, The Wrestler, Inside Wrestling, Wrestle America, and *Wrestling Superstars*
London Publishing Co.
7002 West Butler Pike
Ambler, PA 19002

WCW Magazine
P.O. Box 420235
Palm Coast, FL 32142-0235

WOW Magazine
McMillen Communications
P.O. Box 500
Missouri City, TX 77459-9904
e-mail: woworder@mcmillencomm.com

Web Sites

Professional Wrestling Online Museum
http://www.wrestlingmuseum.com

World Championship Wrestling
http://www.wcw.com

World Wrestling Federation
http://www.wwf.com

For Further Reading

Albano, Lou, Bert Randolph Sugar, and Michael Benson. *The Complete Idiot's Guide to Pro Wrestling.* 2nd ed. New York: Alpha Books, 2000.

Archer, Jeff. *Theater in a Squared Circle.* New York: White-Boucke Publishing, 1998.

Cohen, Dan. *Wrestling Renegades: An In-Depth Look at Today's Superstars of Pro Wrestling.* New York: Archway, 1999.

For Further Reading

Hofstede, David. *Slammin': Wrestling's Greatest Heroes and Villains.* New York: ECW Press, 1999.

Mazer, Sharon. *Professional Wrestling: Sport and Spectacle.* Jackson, MS: University Press of Mississippi, 1998.

Myers, Robert. *The Professional Wrestling Trivia Book.* Boston, MA: Branden Books, 1999.

Works Cited

Basil, Dr. Sidney M. "Hall Is Crying Out for Nash's Friendship." *The Wrestler*, March, 1999, pp. 58–61.

Burkett, Harry. "Kevin Nash & Hollywood Hogan: The Untold Story of Why They

Never Kliqued." *The Wrestler,* September, 1998, pp. 48–51.

"Far From The Spotlight, Kevin Nash—Champion Dad—Reigns." *Wrestling True Life Stories,* Winter, 1998, pp. 26–37.

"Hogan Betrays WCW, Joins Razor and Diesel." *Pro Wrestling Illustrated Weekly,* July 22, 1996, p. 1.

"Q&A: Kevin Nash." *The Wrestler,* Holiday, 1999, pp. 20–23.

Rosenbaum, Dave. "Nash & Hall: Survey Says They're Not Long For The NWO." *Wrestler Digest,* Fall, 1998, pp. 84–89.

Index

B
battle royal, 36, 76, 77
Benoit, Chris, 67, 88, 91
Bischoff, Eric, 7–8, 56, 57, 63, 65, 70, 73, 92

F
Flair, Ric, 68, 81, 92, 93, 94

G
Giant, the, 61, 67, 69–70, 72, 75, 77
Goldberg, Bill, 24, 77–80, 86–87, 88, 89, 90, 94

H
Hall, Scott (Razor Ramon), 5–6, 7–10, 33, 37–39, 42, 43, 55, 56, 57, 60, 61–65, 68, 69–70, 73–77, 80–81, 86–88, 90, 92, 95
Hart, Bret, 40–41, 48, 52–53, 55, 81, 87–88, 89, 90
Hart, Owen, 36, 43, 48, 51, 54, 81

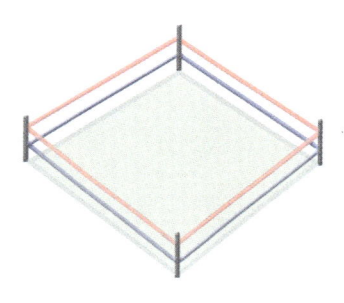

Hogan, Hulk, 9–10, 60–61, 65, 71, 72–73, 75, 80–81, 83–85, 92

J
Jannetty, Marty, 30, 31, 33
Jarrett, Jeff, 43, 48, 67, 89, 90, 91, 92, 93, 94, 96

M
Master Blasters, 22, 23–24
Michaels, Shawn, 30–33, 37, 38–39, 41–42, 43–44, 45, 48–49, 51, 54

N
Nash, Kevin
    as Diesel, 5–6, 7–8, 11, 32–33, 36–44, 45–56, 98
    family of, 12–16, 17, 18
    injuries suffered, 20, 50, 69, 92
    as Master Blaster Steel, 6, 22, 23, 98

as Oz, 6, 24–28
as Shawn Michaels's bodyguard, 31–33, 39, 41
titles won, 7, 39, 42, 47, 63, 80, 90, 93, 96, 98
as Vinnie Vegas, 6, 28–29
National Wrestling Alliance (NWA), 22
New World Order (NWO), 10, 11, 61, 63–68, 69, 70–71, 63–71, 81, 83, 90, 98
NWO Hollywood, 73, 75, 76
NWO Wolfpac, 73, 75, 76, 77
Niedhart, Jim, 40–41, 43
Nitro, 61, 64, 71, 73, 76, 77, 83, 86, 87, 88, 89, 90, 92, 93–94, 95, 96, 98

O
Outsiders, the, 8–9, 56, 60, 80, 89

P
Page, Diamond Dallas, 29, 65, 81, 92, 98

S
Savage, Randy, 8, 9, 33, 60, 65, 73, 75, 81, 82, 83
Smith, Davey Boy, 43, 51, 52
Steiner, Scott, 21, 36–37, 64–65, 67, 69, 81, 93, 94–95
Sting, 8, 9, 10, 60, 69, 70, 71, 75, 82–83, 92

W
World Championship Wrestling (WCW), 6, 7, 8, 10, 11, 25, 27, 28, 29, 31, 44, 48, 56, 57, 61, 63–64, 65, 67, 68, 69, 71, 73, 77, 80, 85, 88, 89, 90, 91, 92, 93, 95
World Wrestling Federation (WWF), 5–6, 7, 8, 11, 21, 30, 31, 33, 36, 38, 40, 41, 45, 47, 48, 51, 53, 55–56, 60, 64, 77, 81, 98
WrestleMania, 36, 37, 48, 54

Photo Credits
All photos © Colin Bowman.

Series Design and Layout
Geri Giordano